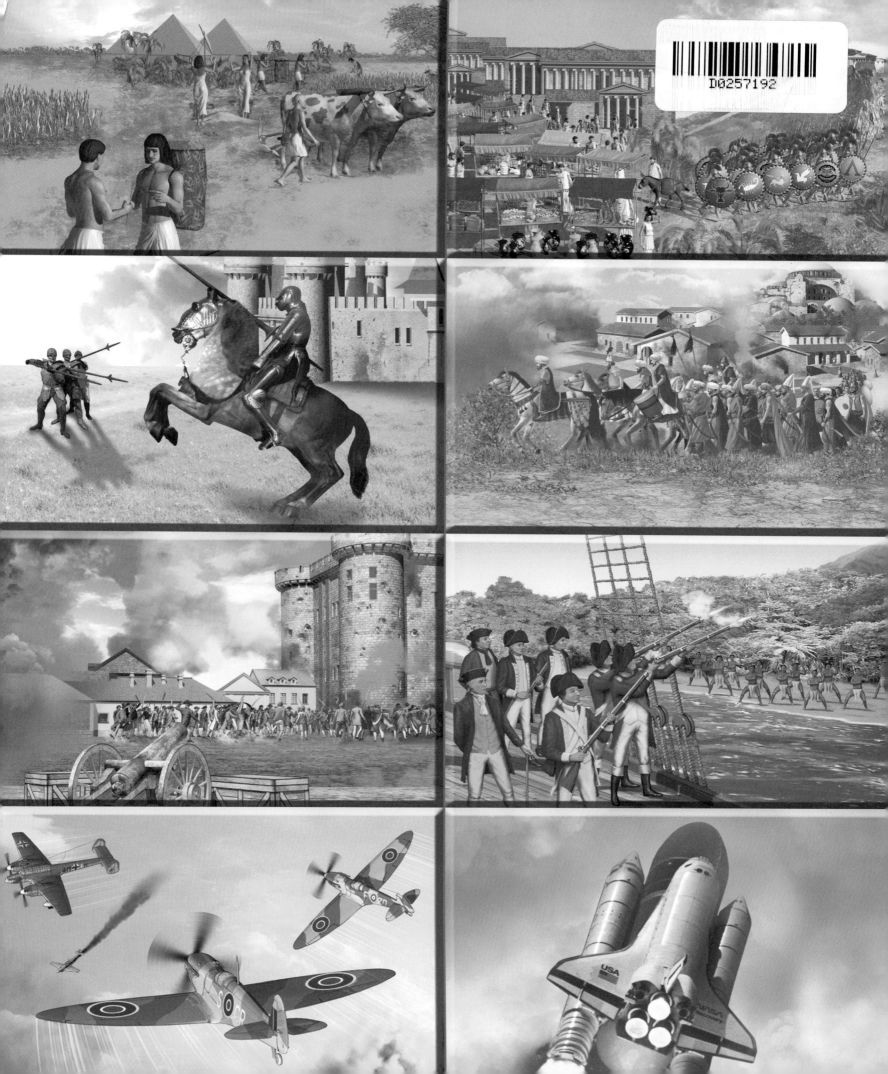

PRIMARY EXPLORERS
HISTORY
THROUGH THE AGES

igloobooks

Contents

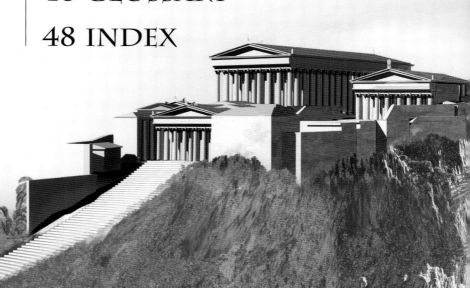

LOOKING AT THE PAST

LOOKING AT THE PAST TIMELINE

4.6 billion years ago
The Earth is formed.

3,500 million years ago (MYA)
The first life forms appear on Earth.

570 MYA Complex creatures emerge.

245–65 MYA (Mesozoic era)
The world is ruled by giant reptiles.

65 MYA (Cenozoic era)
Mammals first appear.

4 MYA The earliest form of humans emerge, called hominids.

2 MYA Homo erectus (upright man) appears.

160,000 years ago
Homo sapiens evolve from Homo erectus.

120,000 BC A primitive people called Neanderthals live in European caves.

110,000 BC The Ice Age begins.

35,000 years ago
Neanderthals die out, and Homo sapiens migrate across the globe.

People adapted to living in the ice age by becoming expert hunters.

History is the story of human beings and the events of our past. Human history may seem long, but it is short compared to the life of our planet.

Humans like us have existed for around 160,000 years, but the Earth is 4.6 billion years old. We measure history using two time periods – BC and AD. BC is everything that happened before the year 0. AD is everything that came after.

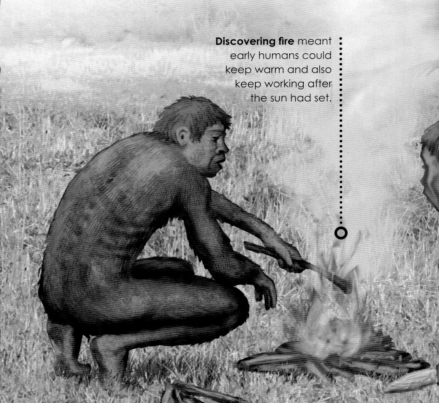

Discovering fire meant early humans could keep warm and also keep working after the sun had set.

Early humans made tools so that they could dig for roots and smash hard objects

PRE-HISTORY

Life on Earth began around 3,500 million years ago. Over time, different creatures appeared, evolved and then became extinct. Around 245 million years ago, giant dinosaurs walked the Earth. Then, 65 million years ago, the dinosaurs were wiped out and mammals took over. One type of mammal that appeared at this time – the ape – would eventually evolve into humans.

EARLY HUMANS

The technical name for modern humans is 'Homo sapien' – meaning 'the wise human' in latin. Homo sapiens evolved from Homo erectus, which means 'upright man'. These early humans lived two million years ago in Africa. Here, they led simple lives hunting animals and gathering plants for food. They made basic tools from stone and wood and lived in caves. Eventually, Homo erectus left Africa and became Homo sapiens – the humans we are today.

DID YOU KNOW?

Archaeology is the study of human history by digging up objects from the past.

HOW DO WE KNOW?

We learn about history by studying the things people have left behind. These include stone tools from Africa, wall paintings on ancient Egyptian tombs and whole Roman cities buried underground. Writing from the past has also been discovered, too. Every year we uncover more of our history.

Early humans used sharpened stones to tear flesh from dead animals

Eating meat gave early humans more energy to explore and travel to new areas.

Billions of years ago the Earth had one joined-up continent called Pangaea. Over millions of years, Pangaea broke up into the continents we live on today.

EARLY CIVILIZATIONS

Around 10,000 years ago, the climate on Earth became wetter and warmer. Humans began to settle in one place and developed the first farms.

People had discovered they could grow crops by planting seeds in the ground. They also realized they could tame animals, such as sheep, for their meat, skin and milk. For the first time, people had more than enough food. They now had spare time to build homes, weave cloth and make pots.

MESOPOTAMIA

The first cities sprang up in a region between the Euphrates and Tigris rivers, called Mesopotamia. Mesopotamia was a hot desert area, but the land between the rivers was fertile. The people who lived here were called Sumerians. The Sumerian people built a series of city-states. Each city-state included a temple, houses, a protective wall and farmland. A city-state was ruled over by a king, who most people worked for. Sumer became the first civilization in history.

Early Sumerian houses were made out of reeds, later they discovered how to make bricks from mud.

FIRST CITIES

In the Middle East and Western Asia, villages began to trade their food and goods with each other. Some villages became rich and grew into towns. The first known town is Jericho. It was built from mud-brick houses and surrounded by a huge defensive wall. Catal Häyük was an even larger town, with a population of around 5,000 people. Their houses were built tightly together and contained sleeping platforms, bread ovens and wall paintings.

EARLY CIVILIZATIONS TIMELINE

10,000 BC The Ice Age ends and the planet becomes warmer.

9,000 BC First farms appear in western Asia. The first life forms appear on Earth.

8,000 BC First known town, Jericho, is founded in modern day Middle East.

7,200 BC First domesticated pigs appear on farms.

6,500 BC Çatal Hüyük, in modern day Turkey, becomes largest ancient settlement.

5,000 BC Farmers settle in Sumer, in southern Mesopotamia, in modern-day Iraq.

4,000 BC First Sumerian city-states emerge, including Uruk and Ur.

3,500 BC Cuneiform writing first appears in Sumer.

3,100 BC Bronzework first emerges in Mesopotamia.

The Celts were an ancient warrior people who lived across Europe, from around 500 BC.

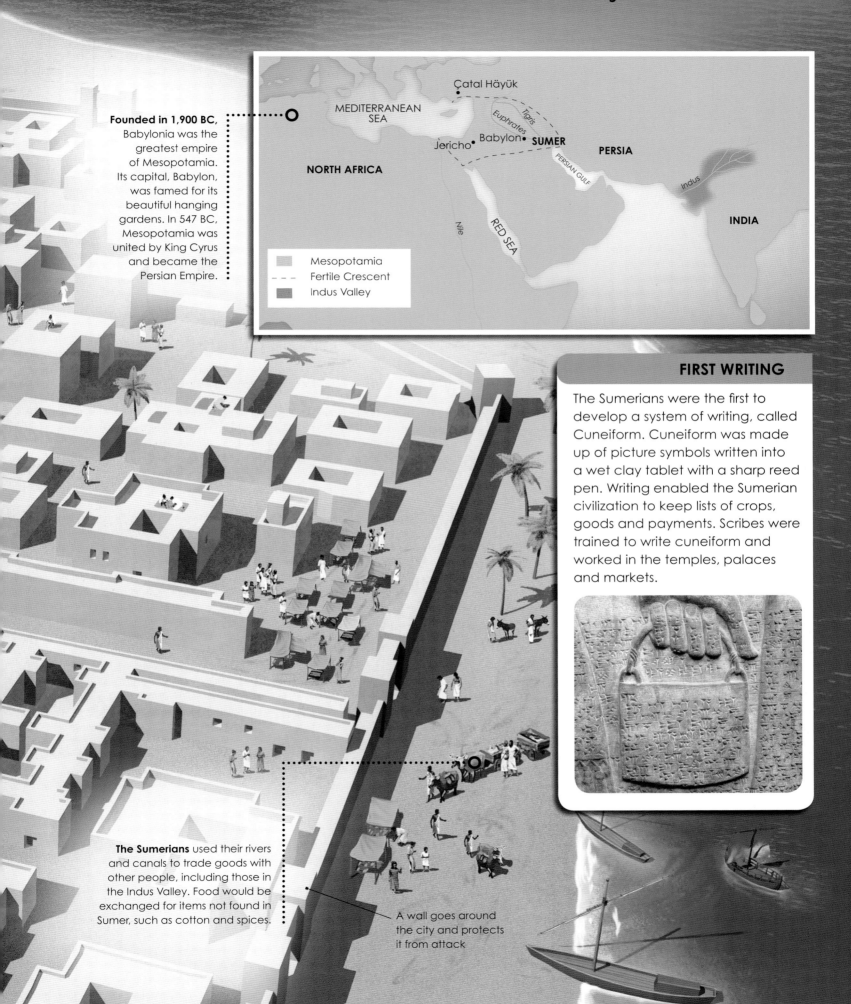

Founded in 1,900 BC, Babylonia was the greatest empire of Mesopotamia. Its capital, Babylon, was famed for its beautiful hanging gardens. In 547 BC, Mesopotamia was united by King Cyrus and became the Persian Empire.

Çatal Häyük

MEDITERRANEAN SEA

Euphrates

Tigris

Jericho• Babylon• **SUMER**

PERSIA

NORTH AFRICA

PERSIAN GULF

Nile

RED SEA

Indus

INDIA

Mesopotamia
- - - Fertile Crescent
Indus Valley

FIRST WRITING

The Sumerians were the first to develop a system of writing, called Cuneiform. Cuneiform was made up of picture symbols written into a wet clay tablet with a sharp reed pen. Writing enabled the Sumerian civilization to keep lists of crops, goods and payments. Scribes were trained to write cuneiform and worked in the temples, palaces and markets.

The Sumerians used their rivers and canals to trade goods with other people, including those in the Indus Valley. Food would be exchanged for items not found in Sumer, such as cotton and spices.

A wall goes around the city and protects it from attack

ANCIENT EGYPT

The ancient Egyptians built one of the world's most successful civilizations.

ANCIENT EGYPT TIMELINE

c.6,000 BC Farming first develops in the Nile Valley.

c.3,500 BC The first towns appear.

c.3,200 BC Hieroglyphs develop as a form of writing.

c.2,686–2,181 BC The Old Kingdom – the age of pyramid building.

c.1,364–1,347 BC Reign of King Akhenaten, father of King Tutankhamun.

c.1,550–1,069 BC The New Kingdom – the peak of the Egyptian Empire's power, wealth and success.

332 BC Alexander the Great invades Egypt and builds a new capital city, Alexandria.

305 BC The Ptolemies rule.

196 BC The Rosetta Stone (which later helps to decipher hieroglyphs) is carved.

30 BC The last Egyptian ruler, Queen Cleopatra, kills herself to avoid being taken prisoner by the Romans. Egypt becomes a province of the Roman Empire.

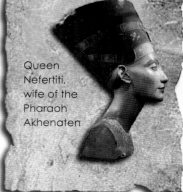

Queen Nefertiti, wife of the Pharaoh Akhenaten

Ancient Egyptians believed in an afterlife. When a pharaoh died, his body was preserved as a mummy and buried with priceless treasures, such as Tutankhamun's death mask.

The people lived along the banks of the River Nile. They relied on the river for water, food and transport. Every year, in spring, the Nile flooded and when the waters retreated, they left behind a layer of fertile soil perfect for growing wheat and barley. Farming settlements along the river eventually grew into the first towns.

THE PHARAOHS

The kings of ancient Egypt were known as pharaohs, and they were very powerful. A pharaoh was in charge of everything that happened, from building temples to making laws and commanding the army. Ordinary Egyptians believed a pharaoh was half-man and half-god. The first true pharaoh was Menes, who brought Lower Egypt and Upper Egypt together to form a single, stronger kingdom.

Farmers gave part of their crop to the government as a tax. Scribes kept careful records of the taxes collected from each citizen.

THRIVING CIVILIZATION

The success of farming meant most ancient Egyptians had plenty of food and lived well. This gave them time to develop other skills that helped their society prosper. They grew flax and wove it into linen cloth, and they made pottery, glass and items from precious metals. They understood maths, science, astronomy and medicine and were also skilled engineers.

DID YOU KNOW?

It has been estimated that 2.3 million blocks of stone were used to build the Great Pyramid at Giza.

At harvest time women gathered the grain, which was cut by their husbands.

HIEROGLYPHS

The ancient Egyptians used a system of picture-writing called hieroglyphs. Each picture stood for a different sound, object or idea. They were painted by important men, known as scribes, on to walls or sheets of papyrus – a type of paper made from reeds.

Cattle were a sign of great wealth as well as a source of food. They helped farmers work the land and harvest crops.

Some 4,500 years ago, Pharaoh Khufu gave orders for a Great Pyramid to be built at Giza, as his tomb. The builders were not slaves, but Egyptians who lived in villages overseen by the pharaoh's supervisors. The huge limestone blocks were quarried, and then brought, by boat, up the Nile to the base of the pyramid.

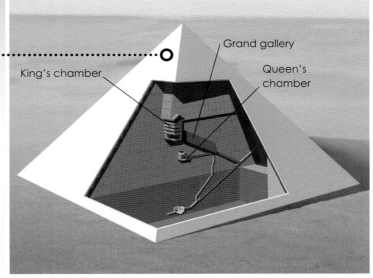

Grand gallery

King's chamber

Queen's chamber

ANCIENT GREECE

Ancient Greece is often called the birthplace of civilization. Many Greek ideas about politics, science and philosophy are still used today.

ANCIENT GREECE TIMELINE

1,600 BC Mycenaean people occupy most of mainland Greece.

1,200 BC Arrival of the Sea People and decline of Mycenae.

1,100–800 BC The Dark Ages.

900 BC The emergence of Sparta.

750–700 BC Formation of the city-states.

490–479 BC Persian wars.

431–404 BC Peloponnesian Wars between Sparta and Athens.

338 BC Phillip of Macedonia defeats Greek city-states and becomes ruler of Greece.

323 BC Alexander the Great unites Greece and conquers Persia.

146 BC Greece becomes part of the Roman Empire.

Alexander the Great went on to conquer large parts of Europe, Africa and Asia until his death, at only 33 years old.

At its peak, ancient Greece was not ruled over by a single king, but made up of small city-states. Each state was independent, but they sometimes joined together in times of war. The most powerful states were Athens and Sparta, who were also rivals. They would eventually destroy each other in the terrible Peloponnesian War.

This building is called a 'stoa', it contains more shops

Greek men do most of the shopping

Some stalls sell vegetables and olives

Athenian pottery was an ancient collector's item

The Olympic Games was a five-day sporting event held in Olympia. Athletes from around the known world competed in events such as running, discus throwing, jumping and wrestling. The modern Olympic Games are held every four years.

THE GREEK ARMY

Soldiers in the Greek army were called Hoplites. Armed with a sword and spear, Hoplites would fight in a formation called a phalanx. A phalanx was a square of soldiers protected on all sides by their shields. Spartans were the fiercest Greek soldiers – they began military training from seven years old! The Greeks also had their own navy. It was led by a trireme ship, which used both oars and a sail to race into battle.

This hill is called the Acropolis

DID YOU KNOW?

The only person to unite all of Greece was not a Greek. He was a Macedonian, called Alexander the Great.

The Roman Empire copied many things from Greece, including their buildings, dress, gods and battle tactics.

Greek soldiers used a wall of overlapping shields to protect themselves.

SCIENCE AND LEARNING

Greece produced many great thinkers and writers, whose ideas have shaped the modern world. We still study the philosophy of Socrates, perform the plays of Sophocles and read Homer's poetry. Many modern countries also use the Athenian political system, called democracy. Athens invented democracy so every citizen could vote on how the country was run. However, women, slaves and those born outside Athens were not included.

Plato

ANCIENT ROME

Rome began as a collection of small, hilltop villages. It went on to become the mightiest empire of the ancient world.

The Romans were great expanders. They invaded massive stretches of land and conquered the people living there. Roman soldiers would turn each new territory into a copy of Rome. They would build roads, public baths, temples and aqueducts for water. The conquered people were then allowed to become Roman.

THE ROMAN ARMY

The Roman Empire was a success because of its tough, organized army. Each legionary, or soldier, was well armed and highly disciplined. In battle, Roman soldiers would create tight, group formations. Like the Greeks, they stayed protected behind united shields and stabbed outwards with spears and short swords. The army kept the Roman Empire under control, as soldiers could march quickly to any site of trouble using the Roman roads.

In AD 79, the Roman city of Pompeii was buried under ash when the volcano, Vesuvius, erupted – as a result the ancient city is preserved to this day.

The Roman Empire was connected by a vast network of flat, straight roads. These roads allowed soldiers to cover long distances at speed.

Roman entertainment included watching men, and animals, fight to the death. Up to 50,000 spectators could watch the gladiator fights in Rome's biggest arena – The Colosseum.

The city of Rome was a large, busy place crowded with people from all over the empire. Every Roman went to the public baths once a day. Inside, visitors would visit a series of rooms, each one hotter than the last. After sweating out their dirt, the visitor would plunge into an icy cold pool to finish. Soap was never used, but olive oil was rubbed into the skin instead.

ROMAN BATHS

THE COLLAPSE OF THE ROMAN EMPIRE

Rome reached its peak around 200 AD. From that point on, the empire slowly crumbled. The new emperors were often corrupt and there were many civil wars. Then, barbarians began to invade the empire's outskirts. In 395 AD, the empire was split into two parts – East and West. The eastern empire survived until 1453 AD. The western empire fell in 476 AD after Italy was invaded by Germanic chief, Odoacer.

CHINESE AND JAPANESE CIVILIZATIONS

China and Japan were isolated from the rest of the world for thousands of years. Despite this, the countries were responsible for many great inventions, advances and discoveries.

CHINESE AND JAPANESE CIVILIZATIONS TIMELINE

11,000 BC Jomon people of Japan make the first clay pots in the world.

6,000 BC Farmers in China are the first to grow rice.

3,000 BC The plough is first used in China.

1,600 BC Shang Dynasty unites Chinese city-states.

1,000 BC First Japanese art appears – clay figurines.

551 BC Philosopher Confucius is born. His teachings will influence later Chinese dynasties.

300 BC Chinese writing is introduced to Japan. The Yayoi culture develops in Japan.

221 BC Qin Shi Huang adopts title of first Emperor of China.

206 BC - 1271 AD The Silk Road, a massive path between Asia and Europe, is used to trade Chinese goods.

105 AD Paper is invented in China.

A tribe called the Yamato came to rule Japan around 300 AD. Yamato warriors became Japan's first emperors. They also brought many new ideas over from China.

Early Chinese people lived on farming settlements along the Yellow River Valley. From 6,000 BC, these farmers grew rice and millet and farmed cattle and pigs. The first people in Japan were called the 'Jomon' people - they did not farm, grow crops or tame cattle. Instead, they lived by the sea, eating fish, roots and nuts.

CHINA

In around 1,600 BC, Chinese farms became city-states ruled over by powerful families, called dynasties. In 221 BC, the Qin Dynasty united these city-states to form the first Chinese Empire. The first emperor of the Qin dynasty was called Qin Shi Huang. At this time, China was the most advanced country in the world. Chinese people had invented rice-farming, paper, a writing system, porcelain and silk. China would later trade its precious silk and other goods along the 'Silk Road', a road built to connect China with Europe.

Emperor Qin Shi Huang ordered that 7,000 life-sized terracotta soldiers be buried with him after he died. They are known as the 'Terracotta Army'.

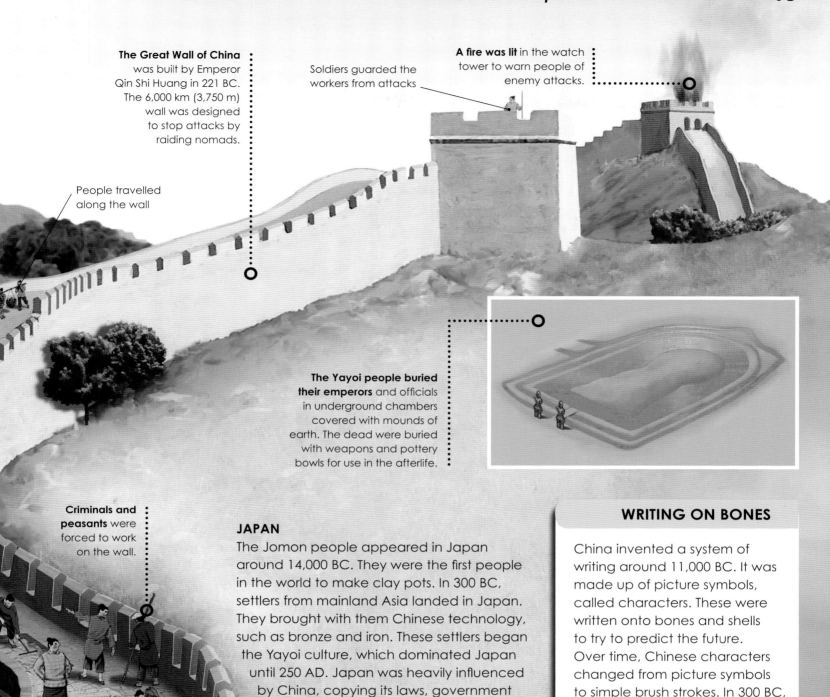

The Great Wall of China was built by Emperor Qin Shi Huang in 221 BC. The 6,000 km (3,750 m) wall was designed to stop attacks by raiding nomads.

Soldiers guarded the workers from attacks

A fire was lit in the watch tower to warn people of enemy attacks.

People travelled along the wall

The Yayoi people buried their emperors and officials in underground chambers covered with mounds of earth. The dead were buried with weapons and pottery bowls for use in the afterlife.

Criminals and peasants were forced to work on the wall.

JAPAN

The Jomon people appeared in Japan around 14,000 BC. They were the first people in the world to make clay pots. In 300 BC, settlers from mainland Asia landed in Japan. They brought with them Chinese technology, such as bronze and iron. These settlers began the Yayoi culture, which dominated Japan until 250 AD. Japan was heavily influenced by China, copying its laws, government and arts and crafts.

DID YOU KNOW?

For thousands of years the Chinese thought they were alone in the world. It was only in 200 BC that they met people from other countries.

WRITING ON BONES

China invented a system of writing around 11,000 BC. It was made up of picture symbols, called characters. These were written onto bones and shells to try to predict the future. Over time, Chinese characters changed from picture symbols to simple brush strokes. In 300 BC, Chinese writing was introduced to Japan, which did not have a written language. After a while, a Japanese version of Chinese, called Kanbun, was developed.

INDIAN CIVILIZATIONS

Around 2,500 BC a great civilization was formed along the fertile Indus Valley. Small riverside farms grew into highly-developed cities with large populations.

Around 40,000 people lived in the Indus cities, which contained granaries, temples and bathhouses. Indus houses even had toilets, which were connected to the city's sewage system. Indus people traded pottery and other goods with Mesopotamia. Then, around 1,700 BC, the Indus civilization collapsed. Historians think earthquakes, floods and invading Aryan armies may all have contributed to its downfall.

INDIAN CIVILIZATIONS TIMELINE

3,000 BC Farmers move to the Indus Valley, located in modern Pakistan.

2,500 BC Small farming settlements become cities – Harrapa, Mohenjo-Daro and Lothal.

1,700 BC The Indus Valley Civilization collapses.

1,700–1,500 BC The Aryan people invade India.

327 BC Alexander the Great invades parts of India.

321 BC King Chandrugupta founds the Mauryan Empire, which occupies most of the Indian Subcontinent.

269 BC Ashoka Maurya becomes king.

185 AD The Mauryan Empire collapses.

320–535 AD India flourishes under the Gupta Empire.

Mogul emperor, Shah Jahan, built the Taj Mahal in memory of his third wife, Mumtaz Mahal. It is made from white marble and took 21 years to complete.

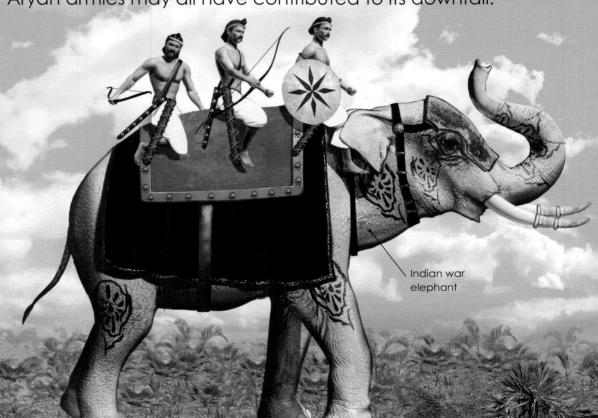

Indian war elephant

THE MAURYAN EMPIRE

After Alexander the Great invaded India in 327 BC, a new empire was formed in 321 BC. The Mauryan Empire began in the Valley of the Ganges, but it soon covered most of India. King Chandrugupta created a stable and successful civilization. He built roads, increased trade and organized a tax system. When Chandrugupta's grandson Ashoka became king, he abandoned warfare. Ashoka encouraged equality and human rights for all.

DID YOU KNOW?

The game of chess was invented in India, as was the art of yoga.

It is thought the Aryan people introduced the caste system to India. The caste system divided people into separate classes according to the jobs they did. At the top were priests and scholars, followed by princes and warriors. Next were merchants and farmers, with labourers and servants at the bottom. 'Untouchables' were considered too inferior to be part of the caste system at all. They were made to do the jobs nobody else wanted. Children always belonged to the same caste as their parents.

Prince

Merchant

Scholar

Servant

THE ARTS

India has a long history of performing arts. Much of its theatre, music and dance is influenced by a manual called the Natya Shastra, written in around 200 BC. It gives advice on everything from makeup, to dance moves and musical scales. Dance is India's most important art form, and has been performed at social occasions for centuries.

Indian tabla drums

THE GUPTA EMPIRE

The Gupta Empire was a golden age of peace and prosperity in India. Many breakthroughs were made in mathematics, science and philosophy. Great literature, sculptures and artworks were produced. Further progress was made under the Mogul Empire, founded in 1526. Influenced by the Persians, the Moguls constructed many magnificent tombs, fortresses and palaces. The most famous is the Taj Mahal, which took 20,000 workers around 21 years to complete.

AFRICAN CIVILIZATIONS

Today, the Sahara is a massive, dry desert where nothing much grows. However, thousands of years ago it was fertile grassland.

Regular rainfall allowed many animals to live on the Sahara grassland. People hunted these animals, and in 4,000 BC, the people developed farms and raised cattle. They painted farming scenes on the caves where they lived. But in 2,000 BC the rain stopped. The farmers were forced to leave their homes, with many moving to Egypt.

AFRICAN CIVILIZATIONS TIMELINE

9,000 BC Kush Kingdom begins in Napata, Nubia – modern day Sudan.

4,000 BC People begin farming animals in the Sahara region.

2,000 BC Rainfall stops in the Sahara, which slowly turns to desert.

850 BC Nok people start making artwork from terracotta.

770 BC The Kush Kingdom invades Egypt.

671 BC Kushites leave Egypt and base their kingdom around the Nubian city of Meroë.

600 BC Nok people start to mine iron.

300 BC Nok civilization ends. Bantu people migrate south and east.

100 AD Empire of Aksum, in modern day Ethopia, becomes a trading power.

The Sahara desert, which used to be fertile grassland until 4,000 years ago.

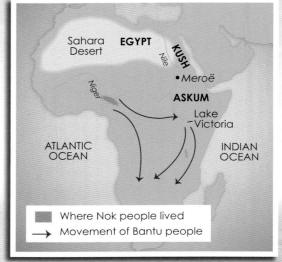

Where Nok people lived
→ Movement of Bantu people

THE NOK PEOPLE

The Nok people lived in modern day Nigeria. They were skilled metalworkers and made tools and weapons out of iron. They also made huge, life-sized statues from terracotta and jewellery from beads. Then, in 300 BC the Nok people suddenly disappeared. No one is sure why. Around this time the Bantu people, who lived close by, migrated south and east. Today, over 85 million Africans speak a form of the Bantu language.

Farming tools were made from iron

A Nok furnace, used for melting iron ore

KUSH PYRAMIDS AT MEROË

The Kushites were a people that occupied Nubia, which lay below Egypt. In the early days, Nubia was ruled over by Egypt. The Kushites built pyramids and lived like Egyptians. Then in 770 BC, the Kushites rebelled and invaded Egypt. After 100 years, the Egyptians took back their kingdom and the Kushites moved south, to a city called Meroë. Here, they mined for iron and became expert blacksmiths.

THE AKSUMITE EMPIRE AND WEALTH

The Aksum Empire was one of the great trading powers of the ancient world. Aksum became rich by trading goods, such as ivory, gold, animals and slaves with India, Arabia and the Roman Empire. With the money it made, the people of Aksum built magnificent stone buildings, massive granite obelisks and even made their own coins. Aksum went into decline from 700 AD, as Arab merchants took over trade in the area.

Ships from India sold spices and cotton

Cloth, wine and oil came from the Roman Empire.

Giant obelisks, called stelae, marked the site of royal Aksum tombs. Buried underground, these tombs were large chambers containing pottery, jewellery and tools for use in the afterlife.

THE EARLY AMERICAS

Around 100,000 years ago, an Ice Age struck the Earth. Ice caps covered the land and the water froze. Sea levels dropped, exposing new land.

A bridge of exposed land joined together Russia and North America. Around 13,000 BC many animals and humans crossed this bridge into America. No human had ever stepped there before. Then in 12,000 BC, the weather became warmer and the sea level rose. The people could not get back to Russia, so they spread out around the Americas.

The Inuit people lived in the cold, arctic region of modern-day Canada and Alaska. They lived in igloos made from blocks of snow and travelled on the water in boats called kayaks. They caught fish, and hunted walrus and seals for food.

The tunnel stops cold air getting inside the igloo

Part of the houses were built underground

The Nazca lines were made by lifting red pebbles in the deserts of Peru to reveal the white soil underneath. Experts think the drawings were made to track sunrises and sunsets.

The Clovis people were hunters and gatherers who first occupied the great plains of North America. They used spears with sharp, flint points to hunt mammoth and bison. In the deserts of the southwest, these early Americans hunted smaller animals and learned to grow crops such as corn, squashes and beans.

SOUTH AMERICA

In 1,200 BC, the Olmecs founded the first American civilization, in modern day Mexico. The Olmecs lived in large villages where they grew maize and made jade sculptures. They also created enormous stone heads, up to three metres high. The Olmecs would influence many other central and south American civilizations, including the Incas, Mayans and Aztecs. In 1400 AD, the Aztecs built massive pyramids, temples and palaces where the Olmec villages once stood.

TOTEM POLES

Northwestern Native Americans were known for their totem poles – vertical poles decorated with carved spirits and animals. There were seven different kinds of totem pole, including a mortuary pole to remember dead family members.

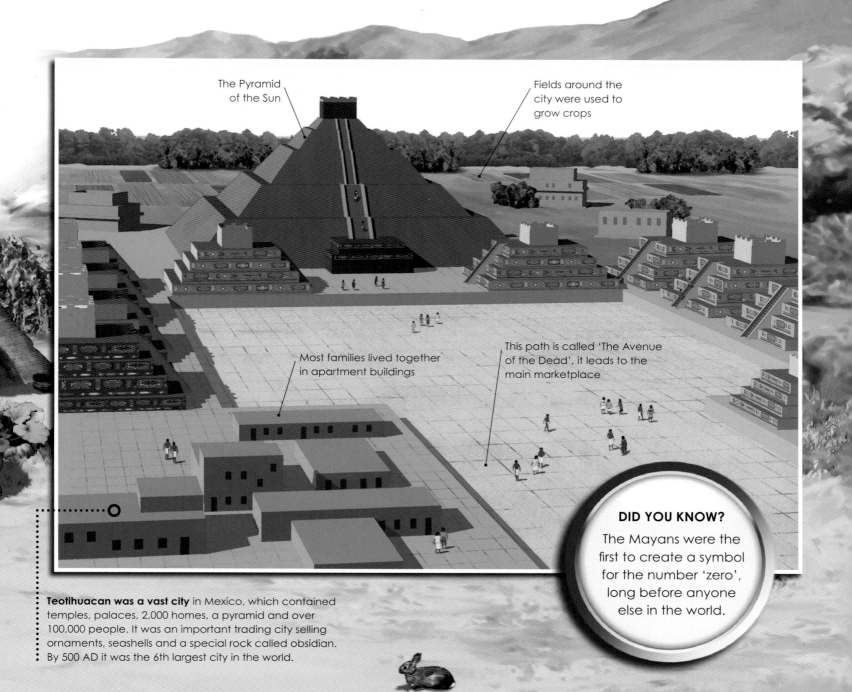

The Pyramid of the Sun

Fields around the city were used to grow crops

Most families lived together in apartment buildings

This path is called 'The Avenue of the Dead', it leads to the main marketplace

Teotihuacan was a vast city in Mexico, which contained temples, palaces, 2,000 homes, a pyramid and over 100,000 people. It was an important trading city selling ornaments, seashells and a special rock called obsidian. By 500 AD it was the 6th largest city in the world.

DID YOU KNOW?

The Mayans were the first to create a symbol for the number 'zero', long before anyone else in the world.

MEDIEVAL EUROPE

The word 'medieval' describes a period in history known as the Middle Ages.

It lasted almost 1,000 years, beginning in 476 when the Roman Empire lost control of Europe. Without the Roman army to keep the peace, Europe was regularly invaded, and there was much fighting. This early, violent part of the period is often referred to as the Dark Ages.

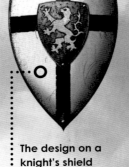

The design on a knight's shield helped the knight to identify a friend from an enemy in battle. This system was called heraldry.

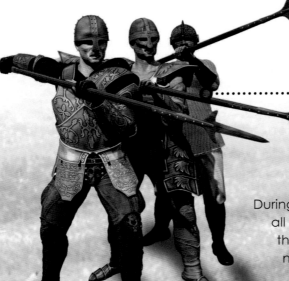

Pikemen were foot-soldiers who carried very long, sharp spears, or pikes. These weapons were usually used to defend against soldiers attacking on horseback.

The Norman Conquest, including the Battle of Hastings, is pictured on the Bayeux Tapestry.

THE FEUDAL SYSTEM

During the Middle Ages, all land belonged to the king. If a lord or noble promised to serve and fight for him, the king presented him with a piece of land. This land, or manor, was usually made up of a castle, a church, a small village and an area of farmland. The noble would allow peasants and commoners to live in his manor in exchange for working the land. The son of a noble was also allowed to train as a knight. These special soldiers usually fought on horseback. They lived by certain rules and ideals (for example, courtesy, generosity and bravery), known as chivalry.

The Vikings were Scandinavian traders, who were also feared as ruthless warriors. They invaded many European countries by sea, in longships.

THE BLACK DEATH

The Black Death, or bubonic plague, was a fatal and fast-acting disease spread by the infected fleas that lived on black rats. Between 1348 and 1350, it killed about 100 million people across Europe.

CASTLES

The first castles were simple wooden towers built in the 9th and 10th centuries. Kings and nobles needed a stronghold to defend themselves from raids and to launch their own attacks against invaders. As building methods and weapons changed, castles developed into big stone fortresses.

For protection, knights wore steel plates all over their bodies. Their weapons included a lance, made from wood, and a heavy metal sword.

In the Feudal System, everyone was a servant – commoners served nobles, and nobles served the king.

THE OTTOMAN EMPIRE

In 1300 AD, the Ottoman Turks began a great empire that would last 600 years. At its peak the Ottoman Empire occupied land across three continents!

The Ottomans were a small tribe from northeast Turkey. They soon extended their borders, taking land once belonging to the Mongols, the Seljuk Turks and the Byzantine Empire. In 1453, the Ottomans invaded the Roman/Byzantine capital of Constantinople, which they renamed Istanbul.

THE OTTOMAN EMPIRE TIMELINE

1300 AD Prince Osman founds Ottoman kingdom in northeast Turkey.

1390 AD Ottomans occupy all of Asia Minor.

1451 AD Ottoman Empire controls Turkey and the Balkans.

1453 AD Ottoman Empire captures Constantinople and renames it Istanbul.

1520 AD Suleiman I, called 'the Lawgiver' by his people, becomes Sultan. The Ottoman Empire is the most powerful in the world.

1571 AD Ottoman navy is defeated in the battle of Lepanto.

1683 AD Ottoman siege of Vienna fails and the empire falls into decline.

1918 AD World War I ends and Ottoman Empire lands are broken up.

1922 AD The Ottoman Empire becomes the Republic of Turkey.

Every Ottoman family would use bright, hand-woven carpets as insulation from the cold. Seljuk carpets from the 1200s have been discovered in modern-day Turkey.

Sultan Mehmet

THE SELJUK TURKS

The Seljuk Turks were a military tribe whose empire began the rise of Turkish power in Asia. In 1071, they defeated a large Byzantine army and settled in parts of modern day Turkey. In the 1200s, Mongols from China invaded eastern Turkey and the Seljuk Empire diminished. Land was divided up between Turkish princes, one of whom was Osman of the Ottomans – and the rest, as they say, is history.

Whirling Dervishes were Seljuk dancers – they were an important part of Ottoman culture and greatly admired by the Sultans, particularly Sultan Mehmet, the conqueror of Constantinople.

A Whirling Dervish.

Ottoman foot soldiers were called Janissaries.

RUNNING THE EMPIRE

The Ottoman Empire was successful because of its military might and control over trade. Istanbul was an important trade centre, from which silk, cloth, porcelain and spices were exported from east to west. As the Ottoman Empire became richer, magnificent buildings shot up in its capital, including the Sultan's Topkapi Palace. Many merchants also set up businesses in the city and writers, artists and craftsmen moved there.

Prisoners captured by the Ottomans

DID YOU KNOW?
The Ottomans kidnapped boys and forced them to become slaves.

Map of the Ottoman Empire

THE DEMISE OF THE OTTOMAN EMPIRE

The Ottoman Empire reached its peak in the 1500s under Sultan Suleiman I. Suleiman expanded the empire across western Asia and southeast Europe, increased trade and governed fairly. The Sultans that followed were weaker leaders who made poor decisions. In 1683 an attempt to invade Vienna failed and the empire started to decline. In 1922 the Ottoman Empire became the Turkish Republic.

Vienna

RUSSIA

BLACK SEA

• Constantinople

GREECE

MEDITERRANEAN SEA

Ottoman Empire 1301
Land won by Osman I
Ottoman Empire 1500
Ottoman Empire 1700

THE RENAISSANCE

In the 1400s, people in Italy became interested in the art and literature of Ancient Greece and Rome. This was called the Renaissance, or 'rebirth'.

The Renaissance had a major influence across Europe. People began to question the world around them and seek out answers. A new age of learning, discovery and exploration began. Breakthroughs were made in science, medicine, the arts and technology. New inventions, like the printing press, gave many people access to books and knowledge.

THE RENAISSANCE TIMELINE

1400s Renaissance underway in Florence, Italy.

1416 Prince Henry the Navigator sets up Portuguese school of navigation.

1454 Johann Gutenberg invents the printing press.

1487 Portuguese captain Bartholomeu Diaz sails around Cape of Good Hope, South Africa.

1492 Christopher Columbus discovers the West Indies.

1498 Vasco de Gama sails to India.

1503 Leonardo da Vinci begins painting the Mona Lisa.

1558 Elizabeth I crowned Queen of England.

1564–1616 The life of William Shakespeare.

1588 Phillip II of Spain tries to invade England, the Spanish Armada is defeated.

The Renaissance began in Florence. It is thought this may be due to Greek scholars migrating to Italy from Constantinople, after the Ottoman Turks invaded.

VOYAGES OF DISCOVERY

During the Renaissance, explorers set out in search of new lands, trade routes and wealth. Portugal was a leading nation of the time. In 1487 a storm blew Portuguese ships around the southern tip of Africa. Captain Vasco da Gama later sailed to India using this route. This created an important trading route for Portugal. Captain Ferdinand Magellan, also from Portugal, sailed the opposite way, around the bottom of South America – he was the first to sail from the Atlantic Ocean to the Pacific, and then across it. Christopher Columbus was an Italian admiral and explorer, who would open the way for the European colonization of the Americas. Columbus was thought to be the first European to land in the Americas, but Viking Leif Eriksson had already visited five centuries earlier.

Columbus' ships: Niña, Pinta and Santa Maria

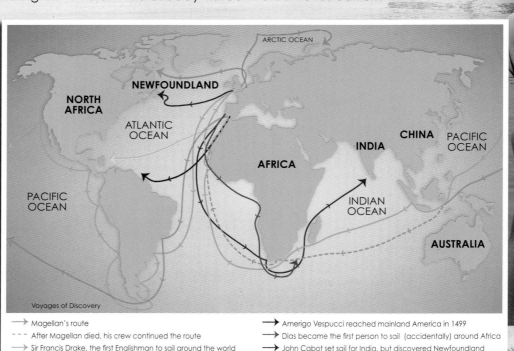

Voyages of Discovery

→ Magellan's route
--- After Magellan died, his crew continued the route
→ Sir Francis Drake, the first Englishman to sail around the world
→ Barents sailed North and got trapped in ice in the Arctic Ocean
→ Columbus' route

→ Amerigo Vespucci reached mainland America in 1499
→ Dias became the first person to sail (accidentally) around Africa
→ John Cabot set sail for India, but discovered Newfoundland
→ Frobisher tried to find China, but found Canada instead
→ Vasco de Gama's route

THE SPANISH ARMADA

In the 1500s, Spain had become rich and controlled a powerful navy, called the Spanish Armada. In 1588, King Phillip II decided to use the Armada to invade England. The English fleet sailed out to meet the Armada for a series of naval battles. In the end, the invasion failed, due to bad luck, bad weather and superior English firepower. The Spanish defeat was a great victory for England's Queen, Elizabeth I.

ARTS, SCIENCE AND INVENTIONS

Renaissance artists searched for new ways of making their paintings look more realistic. Leonardo da Vinci would cut up dead bodies to study how muscles and bones worked. Leonardo was not just a painter, but an architect, scientist and engineer. He even sketched plans for an early helicopter. The Renaissance also produced many great writers. The most famous was William Shakespeare, whose plays are still widely studied today.

William Shakespeare

The Spanish flag at the time of Columbus.

Columbus' flag

In 1492 Columbus reached land he thought was Asia, but he soon realized he had discovered a new land – he called it the 'New World'.

Native Americans greeted Columbus and his men with gifts of food.

Christopher Columbus was so sure that he could get to China by sailing west, that he convinced the King of Spain to pay for his voyage.

DID YOU KNOW?

At this time, some people, called Alchemists, believed they could turn worthless metal into gold, or even create potions for eternal life.

THE ENGLISH CIVIL WAR

Between 1642 and 1648, a civil war split England in two. One side supported the parliament and the other side the King.

For 11 years, King Charles I had ruled England without calling a parliament. Then in 1640, he needed the parliament's help to stop an uprising in Scotland. Before helping Charles, the parliament made reforms to remove some of his power. In response, Charles tried to arrest five of its members. As a result, civil war broke out.

THE ENGLISH CIVIL WAR TIMELINE

1625 Charles I becomes King.

1629 Parliament asks Charles to sign the Petition of Rights. Charles begins rule without parliament.

1640 Scottish uprising. Charles recalls parliament.

1642 Charles tries to arrest five members of parliament for treason. Civil war begins.

1645 Royal forces defeated at Naseby.

1647 Charles I is imprisoned and later escapes.

1648 Charles I is imprisoned again.

1649 High court sentences Charles I to be executed.

1653 Oliver Cromwell becomes 'Lord Protector of England, Scotland and Ireland'.

1660 Charles II invited back from France to become King.

1666 Great fire of London.

Oliver Cromwell was a puritan – he disapproved of acting, dancing and fancy clothes.

ROUNDHEADS AND CAVALIERS

The soldiers who fought for parliament were led by Oliver Cromwell and were called Roundheads. They wanted big changes and for Charles I to have less power. The King's supporters were called Cavaliers – they were often rich people. After several battles, the Cavaliers were defeated in 1646. Charles I fled to Scotland until 1649, when he was sent back to England. Parliament ruled that Charles I was a traitor and he was beheaded.

The Cavaliers won many of the early battles because the Roundhead soldiers refused to travel long distances to fight. Cromwell reorganised his troops, calling them the 'New Model Army'. They went on to win the battle of Naseby, which forced Charles I to surrender.

Charles II was a popular king, who enjoyed music and dancing. He reopened theatres that Cromwell had closed and women were allowed to act for the first time.

REBUILDING LONDON

During Charles II's reign, a deadly disease called 'The Plague' spread through London, killing over 75,000 people. Then, in 1666, the worst fire in London's history swept through the city, destroying hundreds of buildings. Many people think the fire may have killed the rats that spread the deadly plague, too. After the fire, London was rebuilt in stone. Architect, Christopher Wren designed several of the new buildings, including St. Paul's Cathedral, one of London's most famous landmarks.

St. Paul's Cathedral

CROMWELL, COMMONWEALTH AND A NEW KING

Oliver Cromwell was the commander of parliament's army. After Charles was executed, England was ruled by parliament – this period of time is known as the 'Commonwealth'. Cromwell called himself 'Lord Protector of England', which was a similar position to king. Cromwell was a strict leader, who banned ale-houses and even cancelled Christmas! When Cromwell died in 1658, many people wanted to have a king again, so it was decided that Charles I's son, Charles II, should be crowned king. England became a monarchy once more.

DID YOU KNOW?

It was a cold day when King Charles I was beheaded. He wore 2 shirts so that he would not shiver, as he didn't want people to think he was scared.

THE AMERICAN REVOLUTION

In the mid-1700s, American colonies grew tired of their British rulers. They went to war to gain independence and formed the United States of America.

The first British colony in North America was Virginia, set up in 1607. By 1750, there were 13 colonies. In the beginning, the colonists got along with the Native Americans. Then, as the colonies grew, relations became worse and fighting broke out. In the end, the Native Americans were forced to move west.

THE AMERICAN REVOLUTION TIMELINE

1607 First British colony in America founded in Jamestown, Virginia.

1620 English Pilgrims arrive in America onboard the Mayflower.

1763–1767 Britain imposes new taxes on its colonies, including a tax on tea.

1773 Boston Tea Party sees colonists boarding British ships and throwing cargo overboard.

1775 Fighting breaks out between colonists and British soldiers at Lexington. War begins.

1776 The Declaration of Independence is written by Thomas Jefferson.

1781 British army surrenders at Yorktown, Virginia.

1783 Britain recognizes American independence.

1787 The American constitution is signed by 13 states, making them The United States of America.

1789 George Washington becomes President.

BOSTON TEA PARTY

From 1763, Britain forced new taxes on its 13 North American colonies. The colonists were so outraged that the taxes were withdrawn, except for a tax on tea. In 1773, colonists in Boston, disguised as Native Americans, boarded British tea ships and tossed the tea overboard. Tensions mounted in Boston when British soldiers tried to take away the colonists' guns. The colonists fired on the soldiers and war began.

The first American flag had 13 stars and 13 stripes – one for each of the 13 colonies.

America was not the only British colony. In the 1600s the East India Tea Company had been put in charge of all British trade with India. By the 1800s, the company was governing most of India. India then became another British colony.

EAST INDIA COMPANY

THANKSGIVING

In 1620, a group of English people, known as 'Pilgrims', arrived in Plymouth onboard the *Mayflower* ship. Life was hard for the Pilgrims and many did not survive the first winter. Luckily, Native Americans showed the Pilgrims how to grow crops, such as wheat and beans. After their first harvest the Pilgrims had a feast to say thanks. 'Thanksgiving Day' is still celebrated every year in America.

DID YOU KNOW?

The first submarine attack in history happened during the American revolution.

DECLARATION OF INDEPENDENCE

The 13 colonies joined together under General George Washington. In 1776 the colonies wrote the Declaration of Independence, which said they should be free from British rule. After several battles, France sent soldiers to help the colonists fight the British. In 1781 the British army was defeated at Yorktown. The colonies signed a constitution agreeing to become independent states, ruled by a central government. The United States of America was born and George Washington was elected as its first President.

The Arc de Triomphe honours those who fought and died in the French Revolution and Napoleonic wars. It also houses the tomb of the unknown soldier from World War 1.

THE FRENCH REVOLUTION AND NAPOLEON BONAPARTE

In the late 1700s, French people became fed up with high taxes, the rich elite and the king. Revolution was in the air.

Realizing the people were unhappy, King Louis XVI called a meeting of the Estates General (the French parliament). Part of the parliament, the Third Estate, broke away and formed a National Assembly. The Assembly was made up of ordinary citizens and tax payers. They wrote The Declaration of the Rights of Man and demanded that everyone paid fair taxes. However, the king refused.

STORMING THE BASTILLE

In 1789, an angry mob stormed an important prison in Paris, called the Bastille. This sparked off rioting around France and many rich people fled the country. In 1793, revolution leader, Maximilien Robespierre, began the 'Reign of Terror' against enemies of the revolution. The King, Queen, nobles and thousands of others were executed by guillotine. The revolution in France horrified the rest of Europe. The leaders of other countries were nervous about revolution spreading to their shores. Before long, several countries, including Britain and Austria, declared war on France. France defeated its enemies and won new land in Europe – a young officer called Napoleon Bonaparte became commander of the army.

French peasants used their farming tools as weapons

The guillotine was the instrument used to behead people during the French Revolution. A sharp, heavy blade attached to a frame would be released, quickly, slicing through the victim's neck below.

King Louis XVI's army joined the rebels

NAPOLEON BONAPARTE

Napoleon was crowned Emperor of France in 1804 and set about invading the rest of Europe. By 1810, he had conquered much of Europe. His plans to invade Britain were foiled when his fleet was destroyed in the Battle of Trafalgar. Napoleon invaded Russia in 1812, but lost many men to cold and hunger. In 1815, Napoleon was finally defeated at the Battle of Waterloo in Belgium. Napoleon was imprisoned on the Island of St. Helena until his death in 1821.

DID YOU KNOW?

During the revolution, 300,000 suspects were arrested, 17,000 were executed, and many others died in prison.

AUSTRALIA AND NEW ZEALAND TIMELINE

60,000 BC Ancestors of the Aborigines land in Australia.

1300 AD The first Maori tribes sail to New Zealand in canoes.

1606 Dutchman, Willem Janszoon, is the first European to set foot in Australia.

1642–1644 Captain Abel Tasman reaches New Zealand, Tonga, Fiji and Tasmania.

1768–1779 Captain James Cook claims New Zealand and the east coast of Australia for Britain.

1788 First convicts are sent to Botany Bay in Australia.

1790s The first European settlers arrive in New Zealand.

1840 Treaty of Waitangi – British Government takes ownership of New Zealand.

1845–1872 The New Zealand Wars between Maoris and the British.

Maori canoes were long boats covered with elaborate, tribal carvings.

AUSTRALIA AND NEW ZEALAND

For centuries, the lands of the South Pacific lay undiscovered by Europeans. Then in the 1600s, explorers first sighted the countries of New Zealand and Australia.

In 1642 and 1644, Dutchman Abel Tasman was sent to explore new trading opportunities in the Pacific. On these journeys he discovered Tasmania (which he named after himself), Fiji, Tonga and New Zealand. Over a century later Captain James Cook sailed around New Zealand and along Australia's east coast - he claimed both countries for Britain.

NEW ZEALAND

The Europeans were not the first to set foot on New Zealand soil. Tribes of Maori people had been living there since around 1300 AD. Then in the 1790s, the first European settlers arrived in New Zealand. In 1840, several Maori chiefs signed a document called the Treaty of Waitangi, which agreed to let Britain rule. The British Government did not look after Maori rights and Maori warriors tried to win back their land. Many of the Maoris were killed in battle.

Many of the plants and animals of Australia and New Zealand, such as kangaroos and breadfruit, had never been seen before by Europeans. In fact, the Australian platypus was considered so strange that many English naturalists did not believe it was real.

AUSTRALIA

The first Europeans to settle in Australia were mainly convicts, sent there on ships by the British Government. Other settlers followed later, seeking a better life abroad. The people who lived in Australia before the Europeans arrived were called Aborigines – they had lived in Australia for over 60,000 years. By 1821, half of the Aborigine population had been wiped out. Some fell victim to European diseases, while many more were murdered by the settlers.

Sailors fire their guns into the air to scare the native Maoris

FLAG ORIGINS

The Red Ensign was the flag flown by the British navy and merchant ships, from the 1600s. British colonies such as New Zealand and Australia created their own Red Ensigns, featuring the Union Jack in the left corner.

Red Ensign flag

Australian flag

New Zealand flag

The Maoris try to scare Cook and his men away with tribal war dances

CRIMINALS AND SETTLERS

In 1788, the first convict ship landed in Botany Bay, Australia. The convicts had been sent because of overcrowding in the British prisons. By 1868 there were over 160,000 convicts in Australia. At the end of their sentences many convicts stayed in Australia along with the European settlers who had moved there.

THE INDUSTRIAL REVOLUTION

In the 1800s, a new type of revolution hit Britain. The invention of massive new machines turned the country into an industrial superpower.

In 1750, most people worked in villages and on farms. Goods, such as cloth, were made on small machines by one person. Then, new machines were created that could do the work of many people. Large factories were built to house the machines. People moved to the towns and cities to work in the factories.

THE INDUSTRIAL REVOLUTION TIMELINE

1764 James Hargreaves invents the spinning jenny, the first machie to spin large amounts of thread from cotton.

1765 James' Watt develops condensing steam engine.

1769 Richard Arkwright invents a water-powered spinning frame.

1804 Richard Trevithick invents the steam engine locomotive.

1812 Ned Ludd leads riots against the machines.

1825 Trade unions made legal.

1833 First Education Act passed by parliament.

1839 James Nasmyth invents steam hammer to forge large iron objects.

1840 Screw propeller invented for steam ships.

1851 The Great Exhibition held in London.

In 1851 exhibits and inventions from industrial countries, and their colonies, were shown in Crystal Palace, London. This was known as The Great Exhibition.

THE FACTORIES AND THE SLUMS

Coal powered the new steam machines, so factories and towns were built next to coal mines. Young children worked in the mines. People in the factories had to work long hours for little pay, in dangerous conditions. The factory towns were overcrowded, dirty and full of disease. The arrival of the machines had left many without work. Ned Ludd encouraged gangs, called Luddites, to smash up the machines.

Rich people, such as factory owners and businessmen lived in large houses on the outskirts of town.

STEAM POWER

Before the industrial revolution, machines were powered by hand, or watermills. Then, in 1770 James Watt created an efficient coal-powered steam engine. Steam would not only power the machines of industry but also locomotives. By 1855, steam trains transported cargo, such as coal, as well as passengers. Railway tracks soon covered the whole of Britain.

Steam locomotive

DID YOU KNOW?

Many inventions we take for granted today were made during the Industrial Revolution. They include the steam train and the bicycle.

MAKING CHANGES

Britain's Industrial Revolution made some people rich, but many were very poor. Factory towns became slums with people living on the streets. In the mid-1800s, laws were passed to make people's lives better. Towns were cleaned up and proper housing was constructed. All children could attend school, until the age of 12, without paying. Workers grouped together to form trade unions. Unions were banned at first, but became legal in 1825. The unions demanded better conditions and fairer wages by calling all workers to stop working and go on strike.

Factories produced a lot of smoke and polluted the air. In big cities, like London, it filled the sky and was known as smog.

If people had no money, or couldn't work, they were sent to a workhouse. Workhouses were almost like prisons. Families were split up, people had to work long hours and it was very hard to get out again.

Houses were built back-to-back and in rows. There were usually 4 rooms in a house and up to 20 people lived in each house.

People got water from a pump in the street, called a standpipe

Young boys earned money as chimney sweeps, they often had to climb up the inside of chimneys

THE RUSSIAN REVOLUTION

The Tsars were the all-powerful rulers of Russia, who were often out of touch with their people. In 1905, the people rose up in revolution.

In the early 1900s, the Russian empire covered about 1/6th of the Earth's surface. However, life was hard for most Russian people. In the cities, wages and working conditions were bad and in the country the peasants were going hungry. To make matters worse, the Russian Government was corrupt and Tsar Nicholas II was a weak ruler. Riots and demonstrations began in the cities.

The red flag of the revolution was first created in 1917. The flag later combined the hammer and sickle symbols with a red star, which represented the ruling Communist Party.

The hammer and sickle symbols were introduced by the Bolshevik Party in the 1920s. The sickle symbolized the peasants and the hammer symbolized the workers. Together they represented a united communist state.

TIME FOR CHANGE

In 1905, demonstrators marched on Tsar Nicholas's Palace, demanding change. The palace soldiers fired on the crowd. This caused strikes, demonstrations and uprisings everywhere. Nicholas was forced to set up a parliament, but he made sure it had very little power and the demonstrations continued. By 1917, millions of Russian soldiers had died in World War I. The Russian people rose up again and Nicholas II was overthrown. Russia became a republic.

REVOLUTION

A temporary government was set up, however, it didn't help and soon became unpopular with the people. This time the Bolshevik Party toppled the new government and seized power. The Bolsheviks wanted the people to rule and for everyone to be equal. This was later called communism. Russia was renamed the Union of Soviet Socialist Republics (USSR), or Soviet Union, and led by Bolshevik chief, Vladimir Lenin. In 1918 the Tsar and his family were murdered by the Bolsheviks.

STALIN

Once Vladimir Lenin, the man who master-minded the Bolshevik revolution died in 1924, Joseph Stalin took control of the Communist Party. Stalin's plan was to make the USSR a strong industrial power. By 1930, Stalin was ruling as a dictator. Anyone who disagreed with him was executed, or sent to a labour camp. Stalin led the USSR until his death in 1953. It is thought up to 60 million people died under his rule.

Under Stalin, the USSR ruled over many Eastern European countries, including East Germany, Poland, Czechoslovakia, Hungary, Romania and Bulgaria. This was known as the 'Eastern Bloc'.

DID YOU KNOW?

Bolshevik means 'One of the Majority' in Russian. The Bolsheviks called their political opponents Mensheviks, which means 'Those of the Minority'.

THE FIRST AND SECOND WORLD WARS

In the 1900s, two terrible world wars broke out in Europe. The wars would destroy many towns, villages and cities, and end millions of lives.

World War I, also known as The Great War, began when a Serbian shot the heir to the Austrian throne. As a result, Austria and Germany declared war on Serbia. Then, Russia, France and Britain declared war on Germany and Austria and fighting quickly spread. World War II began when Germany invaded Poland and then most of Europe. Germany would eventually be defeated by Britain, America, Russia and others.

WORLD WAR I – THE GREAT WAR

Much of the fighting in World War I took place in 'no-man's land' between the trenches. The trenches were large ditches where soldiers awaited orders to go 'over the top' and attack the enemy. The trenches were horrible places, full of rats, mud and dead bodies. Trench warfare would claim many of the 15 million lives lost in World War I. The war ended with the Treaty of Versailles, which made Germany promise never to go to war again.

Soldiers lived and fought in trenches for many weeks at a time. The trenches were often wet and infested with rats, soldiers had to keep their feet dry to avoid infection.

WWI Trench

Atomic bombs destroyed the cities of Hiroshima and Nagasaki and killed more than 150,000 people.

WORLD WAR II

Only 20 years after the Treaty of Versailles, Germany's leader, Adolf Hitler, had made the country ready for war. In 1939, Hitler invaded Poland and World War II began. The German army quickly invaded most of Europe, except Britain. By 1941, Britain, Russia, America and other countries were all fighting against Germany, which had been joined by Japan. Germany was finally defeated in 1945. That same year America dropped two atomic bombs on Japan, ending World War II.

German
Messershmitt
ME110 fighter

The Battle of Britain was fought between August and November 1940. Hitler wanted to invade Britain, but knew he had to defeat the British Royal Air Force First. Many fierce air battles were fought, but even though the British had fewer planes – they still managed to win.

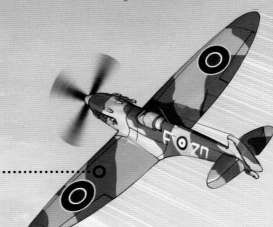

British Spitfire

Failing to beat Britain in the sky, Hitler then tried to defeat Britain by bombing British cities. During this period, known as 'The Blitz', German planes attacked Britain every night, bombing towns and killing thousands of people. Britain fought back by attacking German cities, such as Dresden where 35,000 people were killed in one night.

THE HOLOCAUST

Adolf Hitler's plan was to kill all Jewish people in Europe. From 1941, Jews were transported on trains to concentration camps to be murdered, or used as slave labour. Hitler called this the 'Final Solution'. Camps such as Auschwitz executed 20,000 people a day with poisonous gas and cremated their bodies in purpose-built ovens. Over six million Jews were killed in World War II.

Auschwitz

THE COLD WAR

In 1945 there were two superpowers in the world – America and the Soviet Union (Russia). A long period of tension between the two countries was called the Cold War.

After World War II, Europe and other parts of the world were divided. On one side were communist countries, on the other were Western capitalist countries. Neither side trusted the other. For over 45 years America and the Soviet Union built up supplies of nuclear weapons, in case the other country attacked.

THE COLD WAR TIMELINE

1945 World War II ends and The United Nations is formed to prevent future war.

1949 The North Atlantic Treaty Organization (NATO) is set up between Western countries to stop aggression by the Soviet Union.

1950–1953 Korean War.

1955 The Warsaw Pact is set up by the Soviet Union in response to NATO.

1955–1975 Vietnam War.

1957 Soviet Union launches *Sputnik I* beginning the space race.

1961 The Berlin Wall is built. Soviet cosmonaut Yuri Gagarin is the first man into space.

1962 Cuban Missile Crisis.

1989 Berlin Wall comes down.

1991 Communism falls in Soviet Union and Cold War ends.

Che Guevara helped Fidel Castro into power during the Cuban revolution. He is considered by many to the brains behind Castro's communist policies.

KOREA AND VIETNAM

America and the Soviet Union did not want to fight each other directly. This would have meant using their nuclear weapons, and the destruction of the world. Instead they supported wars between other communist and capitalist countries. In 1950, the Soviets backed communist North Korea in a war against South Korea, backed by America. In 1955, a similar war started in Vietnam.

Satellites are small, unmanned spacecraft sent into the Earth's orbit. Satellites are most commonly used for scientific research, weather forecasting and linking communication systems on Earth.

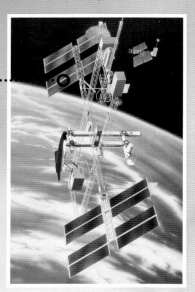

THE BERLIN WALL

In 1945, Germany and its capital, Berlin, was divided into east and west. In 1961 the Soviets built a wall between the two sides, to stop people moving to the west. In 1989, East Germany stopped being communist and the wall came down. Before then, 5,000 people had managed to illegally cross the wall, 5,000 more had been caught and 191 had died trying.

DID YOU KNOW?

In 1991 America claimed to have won the Cold War when the Soviet Union abandoned communism.

THE SPACE RACE

Building up nuclear weapons was not the only way the Cold War countries competed. In 1957 the Soviets started the 'space race' by sending the first satellite, *Sputnik I*, into orbit.

In 1986, America suffered a major space tragedy, when Space Shuttle Challenger exploded seconds after takeoff. All seven astronauts on board were killed.

CUBA

The Cuban revolution of 1956 saw Fidel Castro come to power in Cuba. He sided with the Soviet Union and in 1961 declared that Cuba was adopting Communism. As a result the USA placed an embargo on Cuba, which even banned US tourists from visiting the country. A nuclear war was averted in 1962, when American spy planes found Soviet missiles on the island of Cuba, 90 miles from Florida. When the American navy surrounded the island, the Soviets agreed to remove the missiles.

America first launched the space shuttle in 1981. Space shuttles were unique because they could blast off using rockets and land like aeroplanes. This made them reusable, unlike previous spacecraft.

In 1961, the Soviets were winning the space race when cosmonaut, Yuri Gagarin, became the first man to orbit the Earth. Not to be outdone, America sent a team of astronauts that landed on the moon in 1969.

MODERN TIMES

Today, modern life has been made easier through advances in technology, science and medicine. However, poverty, the effects of global warming and war have caused many to struggle.

At the end of the 1900s, several wars broke out around the globe. In Asia in 1975, Indonesia started a violent occupation of East Timor. In Europe in 1991, the Yugoslavia War began between eastern European countries. In America in 2001, terrorists destroyed the World Trade Centre in New York, which was followed by the Iraq and Afghanistan Wars.

MODERN TIMES TIMELINE

1946 The first general purpose electronic computer created – ENIAC.

1962 First TV image is sent across the Atlantic via satellite.

1963 200,000 people march in Washington DC, USA, to campaign for equal rights.

1971 Environmental group Greenpeace was founded.

1980s Scientists warn of global warming caused by the 'greenhouse effect'.

1981 First PC is made by IBM.

1990s The Internet becomes widespread in businesses and homes.

1993 A racist form of rule, Apartheid, ends in South Africa. Some land rights are given back to Aborigines in Australia.

1996 Dolly the Sheep becomes the first animal to be cloned.

2001 Terrorists fly two planes into the World Trade Centre towers.

2003 Iraq war begins.

2007 Worldwide financial crisis begins.

2009 Barack Obama becomes first black president of America.

2010 Horizon Deepwater oil spill.

NEW TECHNOLOGY

The first modern computers were developed in the 1940s. They were so big that they filled a whole room. The invention of transistors in the 1950s and microchips in the 1970s, opened the way for the first personal computers. In the 1990s the internet connected computers across the world and gave people access to endless amounts of information. Today, modern laptops the size of a book are commonplace. The development of technology has given people more spare time and more ways to spend it. Television, movies and computer games are some of our favourite pastimes.

Computer evolution

DID YOU KNOW?

In 1943, the president of IBM said there was only a market for five computers worldwide.

GLOBAL WARMING

In the 1980s, scientists warned that a 'greenhouse effect' was making Earth's climate warmer. This is being caused partly by pollution, especially from the burning of fuel such as coal. It is thought the Earth's temperature will rise by six degrees in the next 80 years. This will create floods, droughts and other forms of extreme weather.

Genetically modified, or GM crops, were first created in the 1990s. They were made by transferring genes from one plant, or animal, to another so that it would be stronger against disease and insects.

Human rights are based on the idea that everyone is equal. Martin Luther King campaigned for equal rights for black people, giving a famous speech in Washingdon DC, USA in 1963.

Martin Luther King

UN symbol

Even today, there are many parts of the world where people are treated badly because of their race, religion, or gender. The UN, as well as other international organizations, such as Amnesty International, aim to protect those whose human rights are ignored. They campaign for fairer laws and help to free people who are imprisoned for their beliefs.

The internet is huge! We use the internet to find information on almost anything we want to know. It is estimated that nearly 250 billion emails are sent everyday and there are over 250 million active websites.

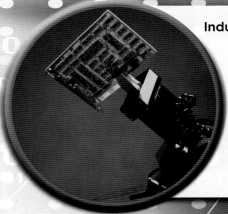

Industrial robots are used today to do many jobs that humans used to do, such as welding, assembly, packaging, etc. They are much faster and efficient and never get tired.

In 1993, The Native Titles Bill gave land rights back to the Aborigines in Australia.

Many animals have been cloned since Dolly, including bulls and horses.

UNDERSTANDING GENES AND DNA
Scientists have learnt lots about human genes, which are made up by a code called DNA. DNA, or deoxyribonucleic acid, is the genetic code all living things are born with. Because scientists know the DNA of certain animals they can now make 'clones' of them in laboratories. In 1996 the first animal was cloned – Dolly the Sheep.

GLOSSARY

Aborigines The native, or indigenous, people who lived in Australia before the European settlers arrived.

Byzantine Empire The eastern part of the Roman Empire, its capital was Constantinople.

Civil War Battles between different groups of people living in the same country.

Colony A settlement created by people who have moved away from their homeland.

Communism A political theory where all financial and social activity is owned, and controlled, by the state.

Continent An area of the earth's surface. Africa and Europe are both continents.

Cuneiform Writing The first known form of writing, it is made from pictures and symbols.

Democracy A government system where everyone votes on how they think their country should be run.

Embargo The restriction of trade in certain ports.

Empire A group of countries that are all ruled by the same government, or even by one person.

Evolution The process of a species changing, or developing new characteristics, very gradually.

Extinct A plant, or animal, that has died out. Many animal species face extinction today, such as elephants, rhinos and pandas.

Fertile land Areas of land where crops grow well, usually because of good soil, plenty of sunshine and a reliable source of water.

Government A group of people who run the country.

Hieroglyphs A type of Egyptian writing that used pictures.

Hominid An ape that walks on two feet and has a large brain, hominids were the first humans.

Ice Age A long period of time when most of the Earth was covered with ice.

Internet A computer network that links millions of computers from around the world.

Jomon Period The long period of time in Japan before the discovery of farming.

Knight A man from the Middle Ages who wore armour and fought on horseback.

Maoris The native, or indigenous, people who lived in New Zealand before the European settlers arrived.

Nazi party The group that held government in Germany and was led by Adolf Hitler.

Obelisk A four-sided shaft of stone, usually built to signify wealth and to mark the tombs of ancient African kings.

Parliament Another word for government: a group of people who run the country.

Peasant A poor member of society, who usually works on the land.

Pharaoh An Ancient Egyptian king.

Plague A deadly disease that spreads fast and kills lots of people.

Republic A country that does not have a king or queen. Republics are often run by governments, or single leaders, who act on behalf of their people.

Revolution A rebellion that is lead by ordinary people against their leader, or their government.

Scholar A person who studies history and philosophy, who writes books and teaches others.

Scribe A person who was able to read and write. Scribes would earn money reading and writing for other people.

Soviet Union The country that was formed after the Russian revolution in 1922.

State A place that has its own laws. States can be independent countries, or be part of a larger country, such as the United States of America.

Sultan A ruler of the Ottoman Empire.

Trireme A Greek ship powered by 170 rowers arranged in three rows.

Treaty An agreement between countries.

Tsar A Russian ruler.

UN The United Nations, established at the end of the Second World War to encourage world peace.

INDEX

CREDITS
Written by: Ben Hubbard
Illustrated by: Norbert Sipos (8, 9, 10, 11,
12, 13, 16, 17, 18, 19, 24, 25, 26, 27, 30,
31, 32, 33, 38, 39, 40, 41)
Illustrated by: Roger Stewart (4, 5, 6, 7,
9 [inset], 14, 15, 20, 21, 23 [inset], 28, 29,
34, 35, 36, 37, 45)
Cover Illustration: Norbert Sipos

PICTURE CREDITS
All images are courtesy of Thinkstock,
except: t = top, b = bottom, l = left,
r = right, c = centre

Cover: Death Mask © Dreamstime;
Space Man © NASA images; Caveman
© Roger Stewart

Interiors: 8t © Dreamstime; 8b ©
Dreamstime; 9br © Dreamstime; 22-23 ©
Shutterstock; 22l © Shutterstock; 22bl ©
Shutterstock; 23br © Dreamstime; 23cr ©
Stutterstock; 13tr © Roman Baths, Bath
& North East Somerset Council;
43br © NASA.